BUILDING THE PAUSON HOUSE

The Letters of Frank Lloyd Wright and Rose Pauson

Edited and introduced by Allan Wright Green

Pomegranate

SAN FRANCISCO

DEDICATION

This book is

For Nella and Linda, who make me a proud uncle.

For my great-aunt Rose Pauson, whose artistic creativity permeated her entire life. She collected and preserved most of the letters and photographs in this book.

For my wife, Marianna, for her understanding and support of my projects, such as this book.

Published by Pomegranate Communications, Inc.

Box 808022, Petaluma, CA 94975

800 227 1428 | www.pomegranate.com

Pomegranate Europe Ltd.

Unit 1, Heathcote Business Centre, Hurlbutt Road

Warwick, Warwickshire CV34 6TD, UK

[+44] 0 1926 430111 | sales@pomeurope.co.uk

Front cover photograph by Ambrose Whitmer, April 1941
Endpaper: Block print by Rose Pauson

Blank margins of the Frank Lloyd Wright office stationery have been cropped for this publication.

Library of Congress Cataloging-in-Publication Data
Building the Pauson House : the letters of Frank Lloyd Wright and Rose
Pauson / edited by Allan Wright Green.
    p. cm.
  ISBN 978-0-7649-5888-5 (hardcover)
1. Pauson House (Phoenix, Ariz.) 2. Pauson, Rose, 1896–1964—Homes and
haunts—Arizona—Phoenix. 3. Pauson, Rose, 1896–1964—Correspondence. 4.
Wright, Frank Lloyd, 1867–1959—Correspondence. 5. Architecture,
Domestic—Arizona—Phoenix—Designs and plans. 6. Phoenix
(Ariz.)—Buildings, structures, etc. I. Green, Allan Wright. II. Title:
Letters of Frank Lloyd Wright and Rose Pauson.
  NA7238.P52B85 2011
  728'.37092—dc22
                        2010041451

Pomegranate Catalog No. A194
Designed by Ronni Madrid
Printed in China
20 19 18 17 16 15 14 13 12 11   10 9 8 7 6 5 4 3 2 1

FOREWORD

Frank Lloyd Wright enthusiasts have long admired the quiet strength and noble form of the Rose Pauson House. It was not a large work, but it was beautifully detailed in fine redwood that contrasted with its massive stone masonry. The first floor contained the studio, dining area, kitchen, and servant's room, and the second floor included three bedrooms and two baths, with a balcony overlooking the studio. Rose was an artist involved in painting, woodblock designs, and textiles. Accordingly, Wright faced her studio–living room with tall glass doors facing north, the north light being desirable for an artist. This also provided a fine view of the Phoenix Mountains. Although prolific in her output of landscapes and other works—created at her residence at 2510 Jackson Street in San Francisco, a house and studio in Los Altos, and her winter house on the Arizona desert—Rose rarely sold her work and instead gave it as gifts to her family and friends.

The entrance of the Pauson House ascended from the roadway and carport up to the house via a long stretch of steps, almost like the approach to an Egyptian temple. At the entryway to the house, a covered passageway identified as the *loggia* led to a small outdoor stone balcony, and then, at a turn to the right, into the domicile itself. This type of entrance is typical for Wright—not going directly in, but reaching the interior by means of turns. Wright claimed that the Oriental mind thought in circular lines, while the Occidental thought in straight lines. He, himself, seemed a perfect combination of the two, and his work expressed a rare and wonderful grasp of the two worlds of which Kipling erroneously claimed "never the twain shall meet."

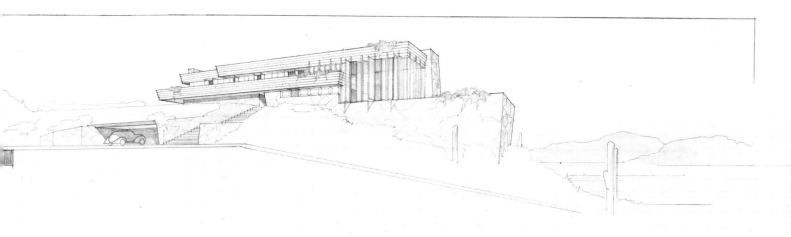

The Pauson House, whose construction began in 1940, cost $7,900, including the architect's fee. Yet a thorough study of the more than fifty sketches and working drawings prepared for the site reveals such careful and intricate woodwork that a cabinetmaker, not a carpenter, was required to execute them. The cost today for such work would be astronomical.

Completed in 1942, the house was occupied by Rose Pauson and her sister, Gertrude, for only one year. On their return to San Francisco following their first winter in the new house, they rented the house to other occupants. Fire broke out in April 1943, and the house was totally demolished. Learning of this, Wright sent the following telegram to Rose: "Shocked and mystified. Investigation should be thorough" (p. 95). The loss of the Pauson house was a tragedy that resounded around the world. Its beauty is now only captured in photographs; it remains one of Wright's best.

Bruce Brooks Pfeiffer
Director of the Frank Lloyd Wright Foundation Archives

INTRODUCTION

The Pauson House on 32nd Street in Phoenix, Arizona, burned down early on Sunday morning, April 11, 1943. The fire was blamed on tenants leaving a tall living room door open, causing long drapes to blow into the large open fireplace. So much effort had been put into perfecting every detail of that house that it is no wonder that Rose Pauson, my great-aunt, did not have the energy to rebuild it. This book tells the story of the design and construction of the Pauson House through the correspondence between Frank Lloyd Wright and Rose Pauson. Although Rose and Mr. Wright became good friends, the letters display the stilted formality of the era. Yet the exchanges regarding bills and leaks are fascinating and candidly expose the strong personalities on both sides.

Rose Pauson was a respected San Francisco artist, working primarily in oil. She also created many block-printed textiles and cards, designed furniture and stage sets, and even wrote a play. The Arizona desert landscape became one of her favorite subjects (the endpaper design in this book is from one of her woodblock prints). Her sister, Gertrude, who like Rose never married, was a landscape designer and gardener, but it was Rose who involved herself in the details of the design of the Pauson house. Fortunately, Rose saved Mr. Wright's letters as well as an album of photographs of the house, none of which have been published before. Because the completed house existed for only one year, there are not many extant photographs. This is particularly true of color photographs, as color film was a new and expensive development in the early 1940s.

Self portrait by Rose Pauson

After the house burned down, the property was sold to Lucius and Jorgine Boomer, who hoped to rebuild the house. Lucius was killed in an accident before this was undertaken, and after his death Jorgine gave up the idea. (Eventually she had a smaller house nearby designed for her by Mr. Wright.) The ruins of the Pauson House were a prominent feature of the Phoenix landscape for more than thirty-five years. They were such a well-known feature that they were given a name: "Shiprock." The site became a nighttime hangout for teenagers. Eventually a street was built through the property as the area was developed, but the ruins of the chimney mass were saved and moved about two hundred yards. They now serve as the sign and landmark for a nearby development. Sadly, that remnant and the materials reproduced in this book are all that remain of one of Frank Lloyd Wright's most creative and artistic houses.

However, the Pauson House does live on in at least one other way. On a couple of occasions, when Rose Pauson flew from San Francisco to check on the construction, she was accompanied by her niece, Jean Haber. My father, Aaron G. Green, was an apprentice at Taliesin West who did some work on the house. He met Jean Haber during one of her visits and eventually married her after he returned from service in the Air Force during World War II. So my brother, Frank, and I owe our existence to the Pauson House.

My father did not return to Taliesin after the war; instead he worked for Raymond Loewy and then started his own architectural firm in Los Angeles. In 1951 he told Mr. Wright that he had decided to relocate his practice to San Francisco; Mr. Wright suggested that it become a joint venture. From then on my father worked on his own projects as well as Frank Lloyd Wright projects on the West Coast. Perhaps the best known of these is the Marin County Civic Center. My father was responsible for the construction of that complex in the face of bitter political battles waged over its unusual design.

My father enjoyed the fact that Mr. Wright treated him more like a son than a business associate. I have only childhood memories of Taliesin and Frank Lloyd Wright, as he died in 1959, when I was nine, but the family connection was strong, and my father looked up to Mr. Wright enough to name me after him.

I would like to thank the following people for their help in producing this book: Bruce Brooks Pfeiffer, Katie Burke, Frank Green, Jean Green, Victoria Hand, and Bill Schwartz. Thanks also to the Getty Museum, from which I was able to obtain Rose Pauson's letters to Mr. Wright. The Frank Lloyd Wright Foundation graciously supplied images of the original drawings.

—Allan Wright Green

Frank Lloyd Wright at the Pauson House construction site

Arizona Biltmore

PHOENIX

Dear Mr Wright –

    I arrived from San Francisco last night and would like to talk to you about going ahead with my house –

    Would you care to come over for lunch? Any day will be agreeable to me –

        Very cordially
        Rose Pauson

Thursday

Dear Mr Wright—

Sister and I just arrived home after taking an active part in the Southern California floods. I feel as if I had been in the Noah family although I cant quite decide which animal I was—

I would like to have more definite information in regard to what you mentioned concerning plans for the house on a three percent basis— Just what will that include? I do not know just when I will be ready to start building but I would like to work on the plans—

Please let me know when you will be in California so that we can talk further about the matter—

Please extend my greetings to Mrs Wright, Mr and Mrs Peters— I enjoyed being with them in spite of the Biltmore party—

Very cordially
Rose Pauson
2510 Jackson St
Fillmore 7638

Monday—

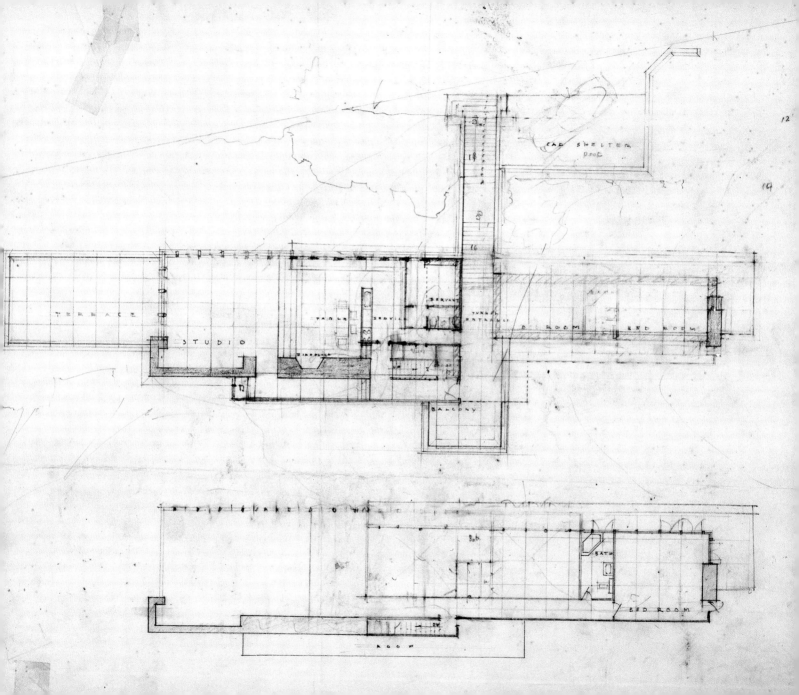

My dear Mr Wright —

    Thank you for your letter
which I should have answered
sooner but my sister Gertrude
has been ill and I havent
given anything but subconscious
thought to the house — I
would like to have you bring
some preliminary sketches
when you come out here so
that we can start to work
on plans —

    There are a few considerations
which we did not speak of
that will probably be important

do you even in first sketches —
I didnt tell you that I personally
prefer the irregular rectangular
shape to other shaped angles —

    In regard to materials what
would be your feeling about a
combination of wood and native
rock? You spoke of showing
me a sample of a native
wood and if you can bring
a piece of it I would like
very much to see it — The
fire hazard in a house that
will be unoccupied so much
of the time troubles me a little —

    I like lots of light and
window space — I will need

plenty of closet and storage space, especially for packing things away for the summer.

In going over my finances I find that I can spend six thousand dollars on the house but no more is available. I hope it will be possible to get what we want with that amount.

My good wishes to you all

Cordially

Rose Pauson

Monday -
2510 Jackson Street
San Francisco -

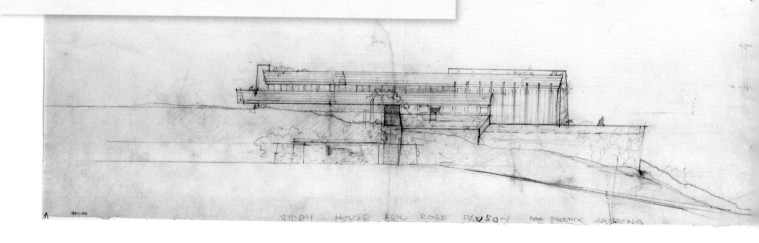

STUDY HOUSE FOR ROSE PAUSON SAR PHOENIX ARIZONA

MISS ROSE PAUSON:2510 JACKSON STREET:SAN FRANCISCO:CALIFORNIA

My dear Miss Pauson:

We are here in the desert ready to build your house if you are ready -

Sincerely

Frank Lloyd Wright
Frank Lloyd Wright
T A L I E S I N
PHOENIX:ARIZONA
January 22nd, 1939

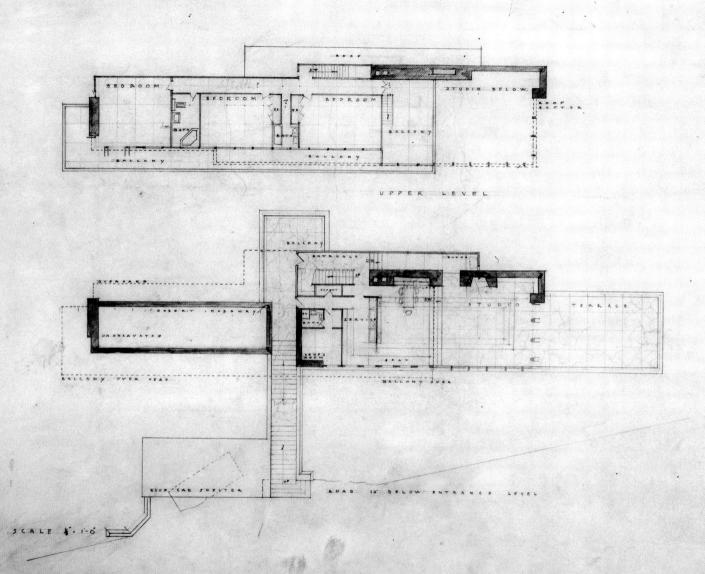

UPPER LEVEL

SCALE ¼" = 1'-0"

HOUSE FOR ROSE PAUSON PHOENIX ARIZONA
FRANK LLOYD WRIGHT ARCHITECT

Dear Miss Pauson: The second stage of the architect's
service has reached some time ago. It is my painful duty
to inform you that there is now $300.00 due your architect,
if you can spare it - he needs it. In fact he needs it
anyway.

We had a nice time the other night - I hope you will be here
soon. I believe you will find the plans, now, better than good.

Sincerely,
Frank Lloyd Wright
T A L I E S   N
PARADISD VALLEY
PHOENIX:ARIZONA
February 15th,1939

14

My dear Mr Wright -

I have mailed the plans for the house back to you and I am very thrilled with them - I am sure that you are going to build me the world's most beautiful desert home -

There are, of course, a few adjustments to be made in your first floor plans - I forgot to tell you that both sister and I are both sinus patients and have to be able to close doors in the living room - Would it also be possible to have a door leading to the inside balcony from the upstairs hallway in order not to have a current of air moving from the living room up over the balcony?

A different arrangement of bathroom doors would be more convenient for me - Instead of the hall door to

bath room between the large bed room and the second bed room, I would like to have two doors, one leading to each bed room - If this allows space for a straight tub instead of a corner one, I prefer it - In the other bath rooms I would like a second door leading to the last bed room - In this bath room I would like to use the full floor area and take the space for the cabinets out of the bed rooms.

One of my personal prejudices is narrow passage ways and stair ways - The kitchen hall way seems to me much to small - Would it be possible to have all the passage ways three foot six inches?

There are a few places that seem to me to be without any light - the hall way outside of the bedrooms, the kitchen hall way, and the servants bath room - The servants room seems to be very small - Is there any way in which it could be given a few feet more with taking anything from the kitchen?

I would like to add a toilet and wash basin down stairs - Could that be placed in the area next to the entrance door and stairway?

And just one more request - Could I have 8 foot 6 ceilings?

My greetings to the Wrights and the Peters - Very cordially
Rose Pauson

Friday - April 29

2510 Jackson St
San Francisco -

16

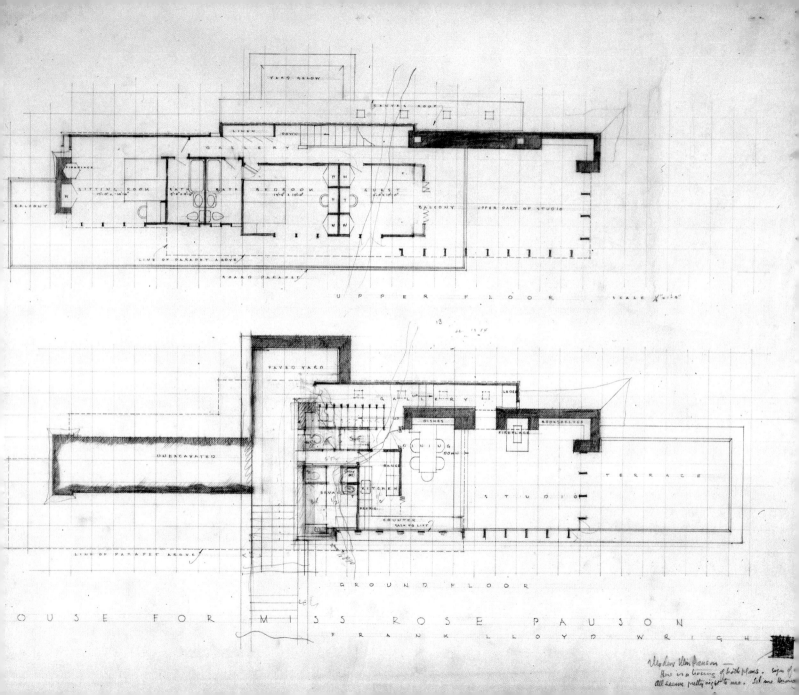

YARD BELOW

SERVANT'S ROOF

LINEN   DOWN

G A L L E R Y

FIREPLACE

SITTING ROOM   BATH   BEDROOM   GUEST
15'-0" x 14'-0"   CLOSET   14'-6" x 10'-0"   CLOSET 10'-0"

BALCONY   BALCONY   UPPER PART OF STUDIO

LINE OF PARAPET ABOVE

BOARD PARAPET

U P P E R   F L O O R   SCALE 1/8"=1'0"

PAVED YARD

G A L L E R Y   LEDGE

DISHES   BOOKSHELVES

UP   FIREPLACE

DINING   DOWN

UNEXCAVATED

RANGE

SERVANT   KITCHEN

REFRIG.

COUNTER   S T U D I O   T E R R A C E

CASH TO LIFT

LINE OF PARAPET ABOVE

G R O U N D   F L O O R

H O U S E   F O R   M I S S   R O S E   P A U S O N
F R A N K   L L O Y D   W R I G H T

Dear Mr. Wright—

It was so nice to hear your voice from Beverly Hills but I was very disappointed that you didn't come up to stay with us for a few days— I also regret that we could not have gone over the blue prints together— Some details that do not satisfy me may be a wrong reading of the blue prints!

I spoke to you over the telephone about the complete closing in of the Kitchen— The ceiling heights in the Kitchen and in the servants room appear to be only 6'4"— The least possible height seems to me to be 7'—

As I see the plans, the toilet is in the servants room with only a cabinet used as a screen— I would not like that— I see no provision for a shower—

would it be possible to change the washroom under the stairs to a servants bathroom and also allowing that hallway to have sufficient width? The closet in back of the dining alcove might in some way be enlarged and turned into a washroom—

Couldn't we be more generous with the bath room windows? When the Kitchen is closed in I am afraid the present lighting will be inadequate. The light in the servants room also seems meager—

Sister Gertrude is making my life miserable about the size of the middle bedroom and especially the guest room. Would it be possible to reduce the size of the balcony above the dining alcove and add to the bedrooms? This is the one point in the

plans about which Gertrude is in arms
and I fear I shall have no peace in
the house if she has to occupy so
small a room —

Could a laundry tub be placed in
the storage room?

The garage shelter seems very shallow
to me — I fear I couldnt navigate a car
into that area —

Has some provision been made for the
hot water heater?

There are a few additional light plugs
I would like, but we can go over that some
other time —

I have had no word from the contractor
you spoke about — If the figure you mentioned
will take care of these things I have
written about, I will follow your advice
in proceeding —

One thing that I dont understand

in the plans is the wall between the
guest room and the inside balcony —
You mentioned a sliding wall that
would open into the balcony — I seem
to see windows on the plan for which
I see no purpose —

Please send my love to Mrs Wright
and my warmest greetings to all my
friends at Taliesin —

Very cordially
Rose Pauson

19

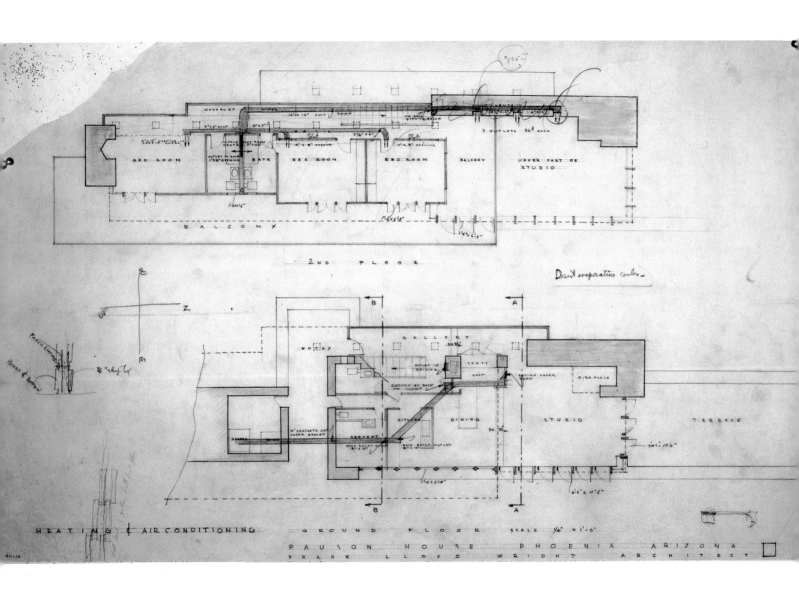

2ND FLOOR

Desert evaporative coolers —

HEATING & AIR CONDITIONING   GROUND FLOOR   SCALE ¼" = 1'-0"

PAUSON HOUSE   PHOENIX   ARIZONA
FRANK LLOYD WRIGHT ARCHITECT

20

MISS ROSE PAUSON:NINE OAKS:LOS ALTOS:CALIFORNIA

Dear Miss Pauson: A copy of your plans went off to you yesterday. I
am enclosing the estimates I arrived at with Ellis in Phoenix when last
there. Bob Mosher had worked with him on them for a couple of months. I
made some changes - included the car port and entrance steps - besides
cutting his original bid down several hundred dollars in the offer I made
him of $7500.00 including architect's fees.

He took it away to consider and Bob wired me while I was in L.A. that he
would undertake the work at that price.   I am convinced that he is able
and anxious to build it with little or no profit to himself and also that
it could not possibly be built for less unless we modify the plans radically.

I don't think you need worry about enclosing the workspace as the ceiling is
perforated and connected to large flue in chimney. Let me know your reaction
as Ellis is anxious to know what to do.

He has built several houses in the region and they are offering him others.

Our best to you both.

Enclose note from Bob that came in with revised estimates.

Sincerely,

Frank Lloyd Wright

Frank Lloyd Wright
July 18th, 1939

Note: Bob Mosher was a senior apprentice to Wright. George Ellis was the contractor recommended by Wright.

Dear Miss Pauson: The Final
Estimate list went to you a bit
prematurely yesterday. It has been
retyped andput into better and
more understandable order on the
otherside of this sheet.

Best wishes to you and Sister
Gertrude - ! (How are the Lady
bugs this summer?)

Sincerely,

Eugene Masselink
Taliesin
July 19hh, 1939

TALIESIN SPRING GREEN WISCONSIN
PARADISE VALLEY PHOENIX ARIZONA

F I N A L   E S T I M A T E S : P A U S O N   H O U S E

FRANK LLOYD WRIGHT:ARCHITECT

ACTUAL COSTS

DESERT CONCRETE	$1,152.00
STONE PAVING	400.00
LUMBER	950.41
MILLWORK	800.00
GLASS	286.00
ROOFING	350.00
PLUMBING	712.00
ELECTRICAL WORK	140.00
HARDWARE	100.00
HEATING	600.00
LABOR	700.00
PERMITS:EQUIPMENT:WAXING ROUGH HARDWARE AND BUILDER'S LEEWAY OR CHANCE FOR PROFIT	619.00
TOTAL ACTUAL COSTS	$6,809.41
ARCHITECT'S FEE	680.00
COMPLETE TOTAL	$7,489.41

Dear Mr Wright—

I was so very disappointed to find that the changes in the blue-prints which you sent me did not include any of the things that I wrote to you about—The height of the masonry, the entrance and the reduction of the wardrobe space in the mainbed room are the only changes that I see. The wardrobe arrangement was much more satisfactory in the earlier plan—

I am sure you feel this house should be as right for my living requirements as it is right for its location—You have done the latter so perfectly that I know adjusting the things I wrote to you about will be only a matter of giving it your attention—

Does the $600 mentioned for the heating system also include the cooling which we spoke about? I would like to know more about what you intend to use for this as I see no outlets of any kind on the blue prints—

I hope you are all having a happy summer—my greetings to all With very best wishes

Cordially
Rose Pauson

Monday—

23

MISS ROSE PAUSON:SAN FRANCISCO:CALIFORNIA

My dear Miss Pauson: Have no qualms. I may have overlooked something -
but nothing I can't rectify. If the house doesn't fit you from the soles
of your feet to the top of your head it wouldn't be one of our houses.

Let me know in detail on the plans whatever you want changed and let me say
how to change it -

The site is only part of our problem - after all!

My best to you both -

Frank Lloyd Wright
August 4th, 1939

Dear Mr Wright —

    Thank you for your reassuring letter — I have followed your instructions and mailed the plans with notes for changes.

        Cordial greetings

           Rose Pauson

Wednesday —

MISS ROSE PAUSON:SAN FRANCISCO:CALIFORNIA

Dear Miss Pauson: Mr.Wright has the blueprints and is completing
work on the minor changes you suggested.

The drawings will be sent on to you again for your final approval and
with contract to proceed with the building early this fall.

We wish you and your sister would stop in at Taliesin some weekend -
we've had a glorious summer for crops - work and all. The buildings
on which we have been at work for so long are finally coming into their
own and we're going to be as sorry to leave here this fall as we were to
leave Arizona last spring.   But when the first snow falls I think we'll
begin to look forward to Arizona's sky and one of those dinners at the
"Suntrap" where everyone sat on everyone-else's lap - remember?

Eugene Masselink
August 28th, 1939

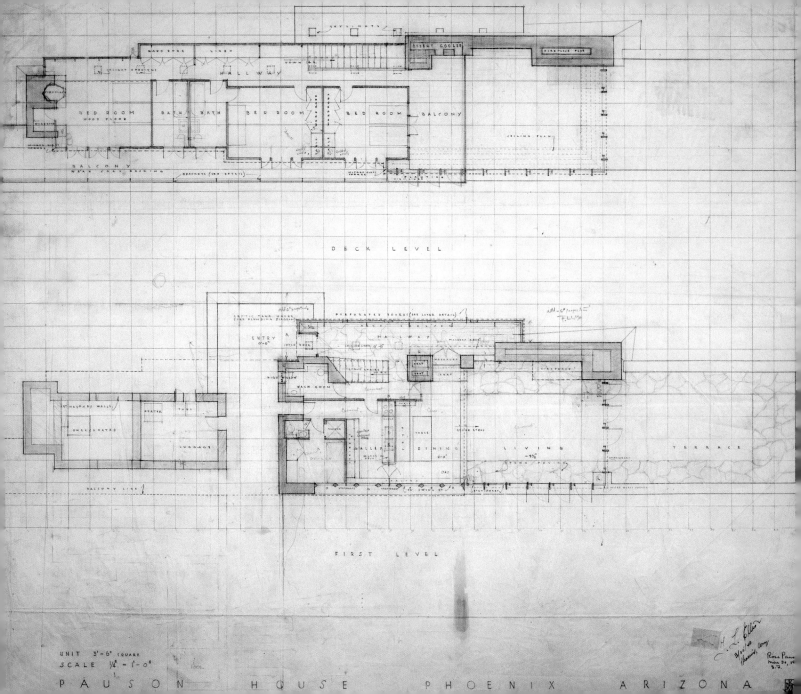

DECK LEVEL

FIRST LEVEL

UNIT 3'-6" SQUARE
SCALE 1/4" = 1'-0"

PAUSON HOUSE PHOENIX ARIZONA

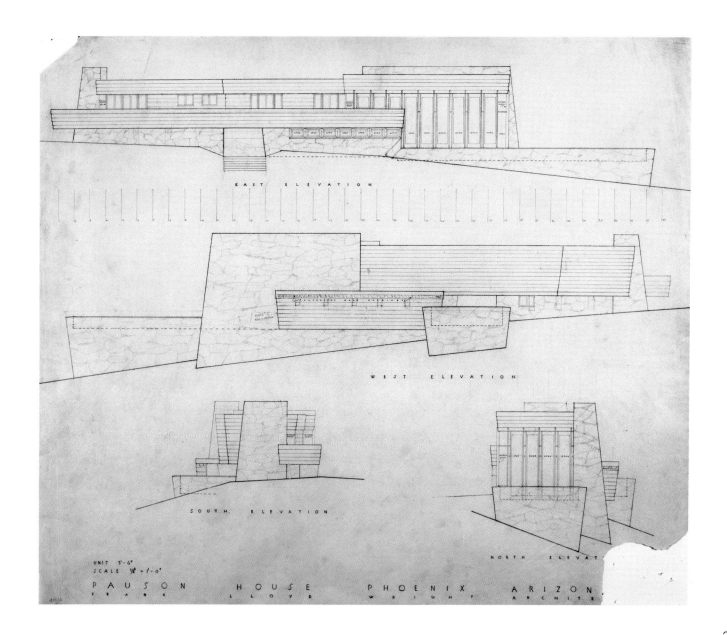

EAST ELEVATION

WEST ELEVATION

SOUTH ELEVATION

NORTH ELEVATION

UNIT 5'-6"
SCALE 1/8" = 1'-0"

PAUSON HOUSE PHOENIX ARIZONA
FRANK LLOYD WRIGHT ARCHITECT

Dear Mr. Wright –

I have considered the plans very carefully and it seems to me that you have done a very beautiful piece of work. I feel entirely satisfied and I am eager to go ahead –

The problem before us now is a financial one – I will have to know what the house is really going to cost. It isnt going to be possible for me to start with one figure and find later that the amount isnt enough – I shall have to present a contract before I can have the money released –

There are a few minor considerations which still need attention – The toilet in the servants room does not have adequate space for use – There will have to be some provision for screens in the long studio windows which will be in use – I would also like to know more about the cooling system.

I hope that we will be able to get the financial arrangements in definite form so that we can proceed as soon as is convenient for you –

Many thanks – With greetings to all my friends at Taliesin

Cordially
Rose Pauson

Friday –

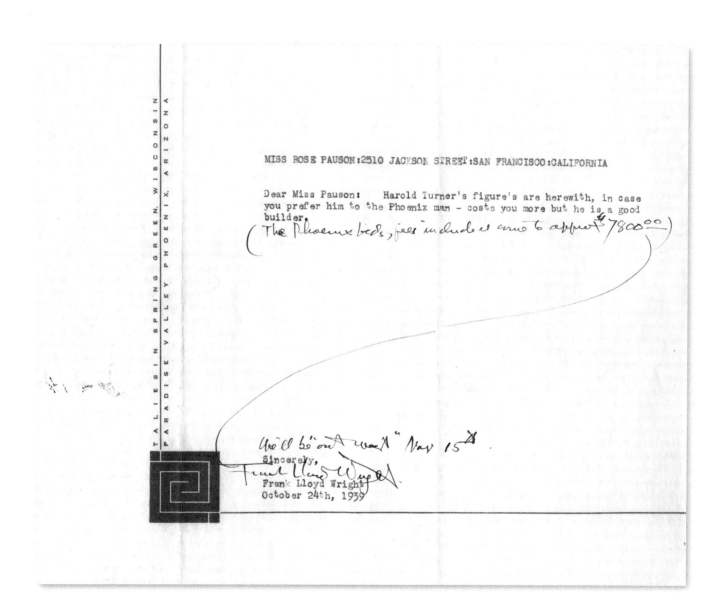

MISS ROSE PAUSON:2510 JACKSON STREET:SAN FRANCISCO:CALIFORNIA

Dear Miss Pauson: Harold Turner's figure's are herewith, in case
you prefer him to the Phoenix man - costs you more but he is a good
builder.

(The Phoenix beds, fees included come to approx $7800.00)

We'll be "out west" Nov 15th.
                    Sincerely,

                    Frank Lloyd Wright
                    October 24th, 1939

31

P A W S O N   H O U S E: FRANK LLOYD WRIGHT: ARCHITECT

ESTIMATE OF FINAL COST

DESERT CONCRETE		$ 1250.00
CONCRETE		280.00
FLOOR SLABS: STONE		400.00
LUMBER		150.00
MILLWORK		1500.00
GLASS		467.25
PLUMBING		708.60
HEATING	407 lin ft of pipe	
	@65/ – $ 264.55	
	Boiler 120.00	
	Burner and Tank 200.00	
	. . . .	684.55
ROOFING		500.00
HARDWARE		250.00
ELECTRICAL WORK		200.00
SHEET STEEL METAL		50.00
REINFORCING STEEL		50.00
WAXING		100.00
LABOR		1000.00
INSURANCE	12%	120.00
		7710.30
BUILDER'S FEE		600.00
ARCHITECT'S FEE		770.00
TOTAL		$ 9080.30

Dear Mr Wright -

It would be very nice if we could have Mr. Turner but I regret that my finances would not stretch to that figure - The very most I can manage is the Phoenix man's figure of $7800 - If we run into more than that you will be visiting me in jail and not on the hill!

With best wishes

Cordially

Rose Pauson

October 28th -

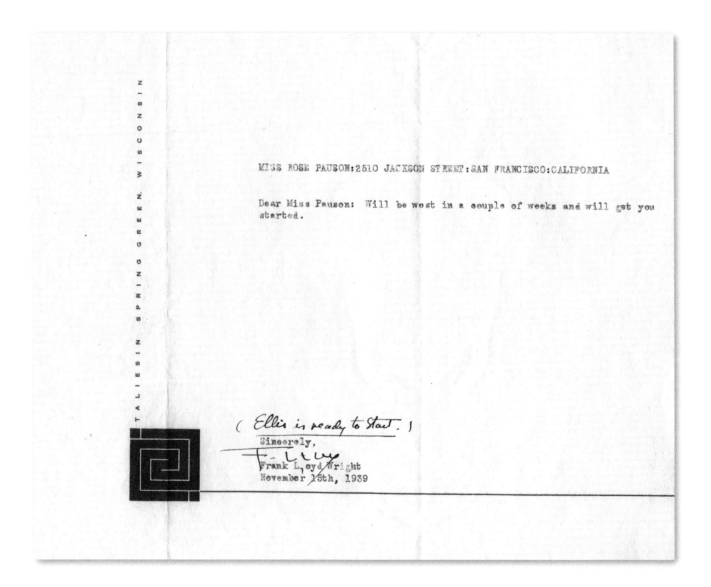

MISS ROSE PAUSON:2510 JACKSON STREET:SAN FRANCISCO:CALIFORNIA

Dear Miss Pauson: Will be west in a couple of weeks and will get you
started.

(Ellis is ready to start.)

Sincerely,

Frank Lloyd Wright
November 15th, 1939

Copy of letter to   Monday - November 27
Frank Lloyd Wright -   1939

2510 JACKSON STREET

Dear Mr. Wright -

Before you conclude any arrangements
with Mr. Ellis for building my house
I would like to recall to you what I
wrote you in a previous letter concerning
the building contract -

My brother manages my financial affairs
and he will not release the necessary money
without a contract on which he intends to
take out an insurance bond. He says that
it will be impossible for me to start the
house on a ~~contract~~ "cost plus" basis -

I hope that this can be arranged otherwise
I shall have to postpone building with the
possibility that more money will be available
at a later date - It would be a great di -
appointment to me to have to do this -

Please let me hear from you and Mr Ellis
definitely on this matter -

With warmest greetings to you all
            Sincerely   Rose Pauson

MISS ROSE PAUSON:2510 JACKSON STREET:LOS ANGELES

My dear Miss Pauson: Mr.and Mrs.Wright and Iovanna will arrive in
Los Angeles early Friday morning and Mr.Wright could probably be reached
at his son's home: Lloyd Wright - 858 Doheny Drive.   Mr.Wright will
be in the desert on Monday and will see Ellis at this time.   And
you will be hearing from them definitely then.   We all hope to see
the dirt flying on that hill very very soon . . !

Meanwhile 2200 miles and trucks and cars and cherokee red paint . .
wish us luck and pray just once, please.

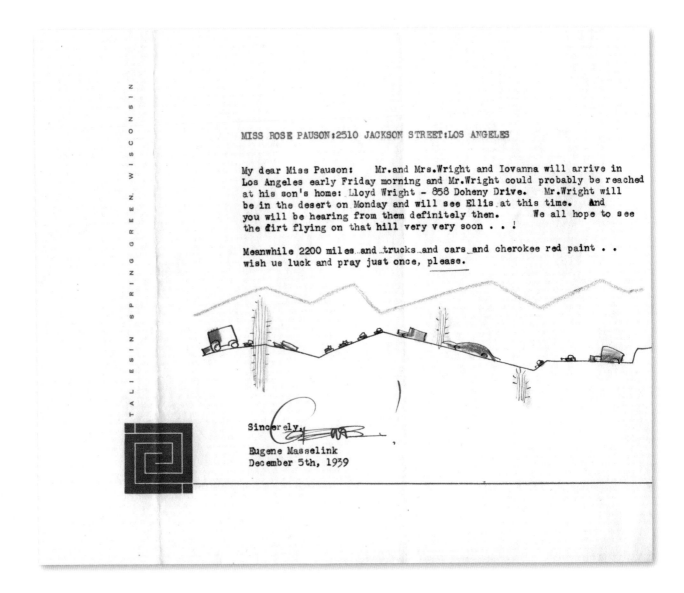

                         Sincerely,

                         Eugene Masselink
                         December 5th, 1939

MISS ROSE PAUSON:2510 JACKSON STREET:SAN FRANCISCO:CALIFORNIA

Dear Miss Pauson: We are all here again at Taliesin West ready to
start on your house . The conditions your brother makes are drastic
as the house is worth about $12,500.00. But we can pitch in and help
out to keep you out of jail if it becomes necessary. Your limit - without
furniture or landscaping is $7500.00 - including architect's fees.

An architect's life is a great life unless he weakens?

The top of the world to you and sister - there troublesome holidays.

When do we start?

Faithfully,

Frank Lloyd Wright
December 21st, 1939

Dear Mr. Wright —

I have waited to answer your letter regarding when we would start to build until after the first of the year business conference — The report shows that it is not advisable for me to start to build just now — This is, of course, a great disappointment to me — The practical side of life seems to rear its ugly head at most inopportune moments —

Please let me know how much is due for your work at the present time — I want you to know how deeply I appreciate all you have done for me —

Gertrude and I plan to be in Arizona next month and we both look forward to seeing you and Mrs Wright at that time —

My greetings and best wishes for the New Year to you all

Cordially

Rose Pauson —

Jan 3 1940

MISS ROSE PAUSON:2510 JACKSON STREET:SAN FRANCISCO:CALIFORNIA

Dear Rose Pauson: What is the matter?   You have broken the spirit
of the Fellowship and set aside something you can not afford to miss.
Your little house was the darling of our hearts and enough creative
energy went in to getting it done over and over again to build a
battleship.

Perhaps you didn't understand my allusion to $12,500.00?   We are pre-
pared to give you a house complete including architect's fees and help
with the furnishings - the dining table, chairs and cases, wardrobes,
bookshelves, etc, (also included) for $7500.00/

We can do this by our proximity to the work ourselves and the volunteering
of a good builder here named Ellis. He is prepared to give you a bond
for faithful performance to our entire satisfaction. Yours and mine.
(the Fellowship)   a little more and then
We could pitch in and help him out if we saw him in danger of getting
stuck.   But he too is in love with the house and willing to work chiefly
for his experience in building it.

I can't see, for the life of me, how you can afford to turn all this love
and loyalty to your little house, down.   Please tell me precisely what
happened.   You owe me nothing . . . unless it is to built the
house - after such devotion on our part.

The weather has been unusually beautiful here. Aren't you coming?

Faithfully yours,

Frank Lloyd Wright
January 8th, 1940

N.B. On second thought you do owe me a box of those
delicious dried apricots - you told me about -

Dear Mr Wright -

Thank you so much for your wonderful letter - It sent me into an immediate reopening of the problem with my brother and the results, I think, are most encouraging - He says that if you can arrange with Mr. Ellis to send a satisfactory building contract for the house he will then come to my rescue with the hope that peace will again reign in our home -

Gertrude has had a bad bronchitis and as soon as she is well enough to gather herself together we will start for Phoenix - Our present plans are to leave here January 25.

Could you get that contract out here in a big hurry so that I can get the necessary business arrangements made before I leave here? Then I see no reason why we shouldn't start to build -

I fear that I have been very inadequate in expressing how deeply I appreciate all you have done for me - Perhaps some day I shall find a better medium than words -

My love to you and Mrs. Wright - it will be grand to see you again

Cordially Rose Pauson

If the boys complain about the apricot diet, don't blame me!

Dear Mr. Wright -

Your letter came today regarding taking over the contract and employing Mr. Ellis - I took it to my brother immediately - He said if you wished to act as contractor and handle the bond it would be perfectly agreeable to him -

I do wish that we could get into action in some way -

I haven't heard from Mr. Ellis since I left Phoenix -

If there is anything I can do for any of the family or members of the Fellowship here in San Francisco, please let me know -

Cordially Rose Parson

AGREEMENT

THIS AGREEMENT made the_____day of_____in the year nineteen hundred forty by and between GEORGE L. ELLIS, hereinafter called the Contractor, and ROSE PAUSON, hereinafter called the Owner.

WITNESSETH: That whereas the Owner intends to erect a frame dwelling on property known as _legal Description "Lot, Block, County, State"_

NOW, THEREFORE, the Contractor and the Owner, for the consideration herein- after named agree as follows:

ARTICLE 1. The Contractor agrees *to,* provide all materials and perform all work necessary for the proper construction and completion of the work shown and described on drawings and specifications, prepared by Frank Lloyd Wright, hereafter called the Architect, bearing the title " ±_____ _____" and numbered _____to _____.

ARTICLE 2. The Contractor agrees that the work under this contract will be substantially completed ~~within~~ _within ninety days from date hereof_. (Probably amt)

ARTICLE 3. The Contractor agrees that the total cost of the work including his fee will not exceed the sum of Seven thousand five hundred dollars ($7,500ᵒᵒ) subject to additions and deductions as authorized by the Owner and the Architect in writting.

The Owner agrees to pay the Contractor, for the performance of the Contract, the above sum in lawful money of the United States of America at the following times and in the following manner.

> From time to time as the work shall progress the Owner shall pay such amounts as are evidenced by receipted bills presented by the Contractor and certified as being for labor and materials by the Architect. Such payments shall not exceed in the aggregate the total sum above set forth.

ARTICLE 4. The Contractor and the Owner agree that the drawings, specification and the General Conditions of the Contract and attached sheet ~~together with this Agreement~~, constitute the Contract; the drawings, specifications and General Conditions being as fully a part therof and hereof as if hereto attached or herein repeated. If anything in said General Conditions is inconsistent with this Agreement, the Agreement shall govern.

The Contractor and the Owner for themselves, their successors, executors, administrators, and assigns hereby agree to the full performance of the terms and conditions herein contained.

IN WITNESS WHEREOF we have executed this agreement the day and year first above written.

Witness .

~~Contractor~~ _____   Contractor _____

_____   Owner _____

Owner

Witness

A D D E N D A

TO PLANS AND SPECIFICATIONS OF HOUSE FOR MISS ROSE PAUSON

Item #1. Workmanship will be good but without so-called finish.

Item #2. The Owner is to furnish power line to the building site.

Item #3. The stone floors and walls will be of rubble stone found, without charge for same, on property owned by the Architect.

Item #4. All wood except floors will be redwood of good grade rough from saw without finish.

Item #5. All redwood to be coated once with soda wash to darken same.

Item #6. Screws to be set in workmanlike manner and left exposed.

List question, etc. you have raised or items not covered by the plans and specifications

Bind this sheet to Contract agreement.

MISS ROSE PAUSON:2510 JACKSON STREET:SAN FRANCISCO:CALIFORNIA

My dear Miss Pauson: Ellis has finally come through in good shape
and all that is needed for a start is your signature on the plans,
specifications and contracts above Ellis's.

I am very glad indeed and know that you will be.   The bond is for the
full amount,(Architect's fee included for good measure.) You owe me
nothing until the house is completed and then $200.00 as the matter now
stands.

Kindly sign and return to this office the papers now in the mail -
sending check for $112.50 direct tothe Guaranty Company.

I regret this couldn't have been earlier so you could see the first
dirt thrown. But maybe you and Miss Gertrude would run over for the
corner-stone ceremonies?

Faithfully yours,

Frank Lloyd Wright
Taliesin West
Box 551
Phoenix
Arizona

March 27th, 1940

44

Dear Mr. Wright —

Isn't it wonderful that the house is really coming to life? I am very happy about it —

I am signing one copy of the specifications and one copy of the contract and retaining one of each — Is that right? I am also returning the signed plans — Am I supposed to have a copy of that, too?

The check for the bond to the Insurance Company is in the mail — I am returning the bond to you as there were spaces to be filled in which I thought might be waiting for the receipt of the money — I would like the same company to arrange for my fire and liability insurance —

Shall I write to them directly or will Mr. Ellis start the negotiations?

I am keeping the general agreement contract — If you intended that to be signed and returned please let me know —

I have made a note on the specification concerning the change of unit which you made on the plans —

I am sorry that I will not be able to come to the ground breaking but I must hoard my resources for future necessities —

I hope all will be serene from now on — Much gratitude to you for your patience and interest in our project —

Very cordially

Rose Pauson

March 30, 1940 —

MISS ROSE PAUSON:2510 JACKSON STREET:SAN FRANCISCO

Dear Miss Pauson: We have all the documents and
work has been started.   Please negotiate directly
with the Insurance Company for fire and liability
insurance.

Thanks for checking up on the error in the specifications!

Bob Mosher is in charge of the work and will give Ellis
all possible assistance.

The House Wing completed is very beautiful and we
all wished you had been here for the several house
warmings we gave it one particularly amusing one with
Marc Connolly, a former Ambassador of Italy and his
fabulous wife (John W.Garrett), Lucrezia Bori, and
others. We carried coals to Newcastle and sang our lungs
out for them all.   But now we are going to leave it
all - reluctantly but happily knowing that the Pauson
House is now a matter of stone, cement, and redwood as
well as of the spirit.

Yours,

Eugene Masselink
Taliesin West
Box 551
Phoenix
 April 5th, 1940

TALIESIN WEST · BOX 551 · PHOENIX · ARIZONA

MISS ROSE PAUSON:2510 JACKSON STREET:SAN FRANCISCO:CALIFORNIA

Dear Rose Pauson: We are still here on the desert but leave in a day or
two. We can take up the matter of drawer space later on if you wish.

We are in hard luck at the first go off on the lot. We struck solid rock —
and are blasting out your garage.   The well is something too.   I wish
you would let me know the exact conditions of your ownership and the use of it
be the people next door. It looks as though a new equipment was due. I am
enclosing a breakdown of costs of same –

Sincerely yours,

Frank Lloyd Wright
April 24th, 1940

*$1097.*$\frac{30}{100}$ *mailed to Dodge Ellis*
June 6 1940 —

MISS ROSE PAUSON:2510 JACKSON STREET:SAN FRANCISCO:CALIFORNIA

My dear Miss Pauson:

Enclosed is certificate for Ellis' first payment.   The car port was a hard
job as we ran into solid rock and had to drill and blast it out while I
was still there.   We should allow Ellis something on account of this but we
can take that up with him later.

They seem, judging by Bob's report to be making fair progress.   There has been
some delay in getting this off to you so I hope you can send the money promptly.

My best to you, and the sister,

Frank Lloyd Wright
June 4th, 1940

A R C H I T E C T ' S
C E R T I F I C A T E

FRANK LLOYD WRIGHT . ARCHITECT

PAYMENT TO BE DISTRIBUTED AS FOLLOWS:

Owner___Miss Rose Pauson

Building_Dwelling for Rose Pauson
             Phoenix, Arizona

Contractor_George Ellis

Work_____General Contractor

Date_____June 1st, 1940

Payment due___$1,097.30

Held against completion
of Building $193.64

Contract Price___$6,820.00

Extra work_____

Total Contract___$6,820.00

Total Payments issued
heretofore_____

Total Held_____

Approved

Drilling	123.63
Power Shovel	186.00
Labor	403.44
Lumber, Cement, etc	393.12
Gravel	43.75
Stone	152.00

Received payment

MISS ROSE PAUSON "25I0 JACKSON STREET: SAN FRANCISCO:

DEAR MISS PAUSON:

Enclosed find the Guaranty Bond which was forewarded
to me from Taliesin in Wisconsin. Also there is included acopy of the Specifications and a copy of the
Contract both signed by George Ellis for you to sign
and returnto me or toMr Ellis, directly , for his files.

The new Gould Pump will indeed be a luxury for the mixing
of cement forwe have been handicapped somewhat bythe
lack of water. I'msure that you will findthe pump satisfactory, it isthe same make and supplied by the same
concern that installed our pump here inthe Desert. They
have given usthe best ofservice and the system hasgiven
us little or no trouble.

The large chimney mass is slowlybeing finished to itstop,
it raisesto the great height of 28 feet above ground. Wish
you could see the ramp that leads tothe topof the chimney
from the ground, its quite a tressle-like structure.

Sincerely,

Robert Mosher
June 6th I940

51

Dear Mr Wright—

I am sending a sample of floor covering for the living room for your approval— Will you mail it back to me as soon as possible? I had to practically pry it away from the salesman and promised to return it very soon. I have covered the field very thoroughly and this

is the carpet I think is best— I hope you will like it— I am not using any wool in the house as I am sure the moths and bugs will get the best of me during the Summer—

Here comes another problem— I like your idea of carrying the rug through the terrace area— However it appears that nothing made for indoor use will hold up when used outdoors— I can't work on the theory that it can be rolled up and put

away because it will be more in the
way of service than I expect to have
out there. The salesman assured me
that rugs made for indoors would not
stand the Arizona sun outdoors - Also the
expense of carpeting the terraces in this
material would stop me -

What would you think of using a
sisal material or a Chinese matting
in natural color for the outdoors? It
would carry the color straight through -

It will take a month to make the rug
and I would like to order it as soon
as possible if you approve of it -
I am feeling quite excited about the
house and hope I can hold together
without exploding until I see it!
My love and greetings to you all
Cordially
Rose Pauson

Friday -

53

TALIESIN SPRING GREEN, WISCONSIN

MISS ROSE PAUSON:2510 JACKSON STREET:SAN FRANCISCO:CALIFORNIA

Dear Miss Pauson: Herewith the second Architect's Certificate approved
by Mr.Wright and ready for payment.

We're all happy and busy -- in Wisconsin, Maryland, Massachusetts, Florida,
Missouri, Illinois, Alabama, California, _and_ Arizona.   How are you?

Best regards --

GENE

Eugene Masselink
Secretary to Frank Lloyd Wright
July 10th, 1940

54

Dear Mr. Wright –

Would it be possible to postpone the decision about the drawer space and shelves until I land in Arizona and see the finished rooms? I am very much intrigued by the lovely drawings which you sent me but I am afraid that the open shelves won't look like the picture when piled with nightgowns and stockings and the various what nots that make a ladies' existence a nuisance. I will keep the plans until I hear from you – If you want my decision now I shall work on it and return the plans –

I hope the Fellowship had a safe trip back to Wisconsin – My greetings to all –

I am delighted that Bob Mosher is going to nurse my house along –

Greetings to all the family
Cordially
Rose Pauson

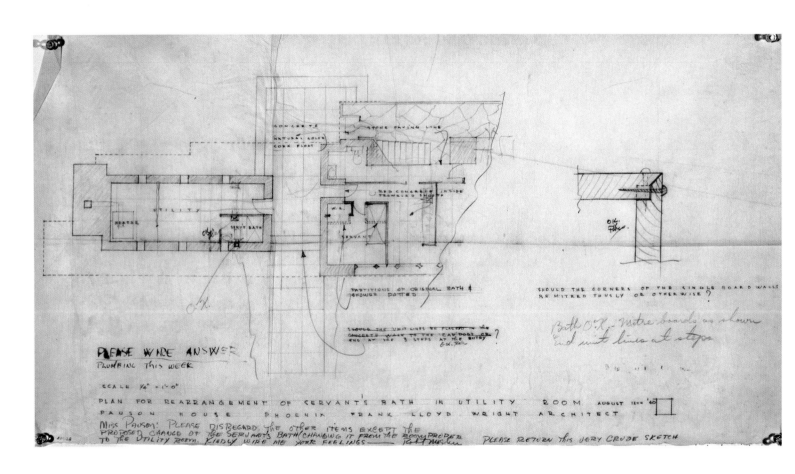

PLEASE WIRE ANSWER
PLUMBING THIS WEEK

SCALE ¼" = 1'-0"

PLAN FOR REARRANGEMENT OF SERVANTS BATH IN UTILITY ROOM AUGUST 12th '40

PAUSON HOUSE PHOENIX FRANK LLOYD WRIGHT ARCHITECT

MISS PAUSON: PLEASE DISREGARD THE OTHER ITEMS EXCEPT THE
PROPOSED CHANGE OF THE SERVANTS BATH CHANGING IT FROM THE ROOM PROPER
TO THE UTILITY ROOM. KINDLY WIRE ME YOUR FEELINGS — Port master   PLEASE RETURN THIS VERY CRUDE SKETCH

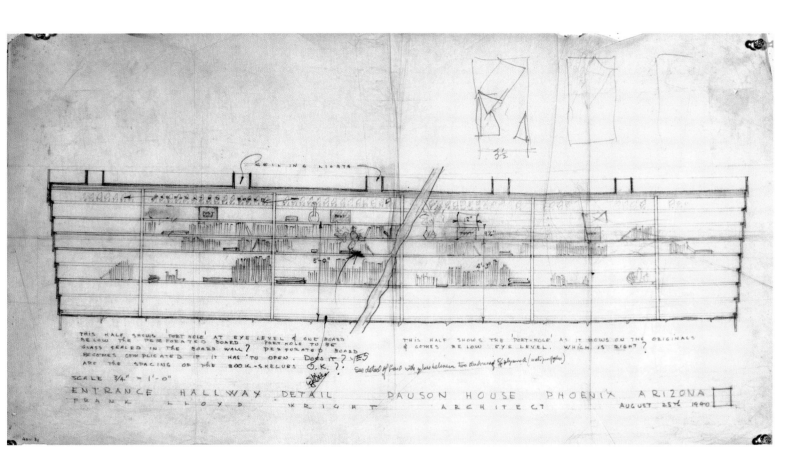

THIS HALF SHOWS 'PORT HOLE' AT EYE LEVEL & ONE BOARD
BELOW THE PERFORATED BOARD. PORTHOLE TO BE
GLASS SEALED IN THE BOARD WALL? PERFORATED BOARD
BECOMES COMPLICATED IF IT HAS TO OPEN. DOES IT? YES
ARE THE SPACING OF THE BOOK-SHELVES O.K. ?

THIS HALF SHOWS THE 'PORT-HOLE' AS IT SHOWS ON THE ORIGINALS
& COMES BELOW EYE LEVEL. WHICH IS RIGHT ?

See detail of hand with glass between two thicknesses of plywood (metal grip plates)

SCALE 3/4" = 1'-0"

ENTRANCE HALLWAY DETAIL   DAUSON HOUSE PHOENIX ARIZONA
FRANK   LLOYD   WRIGHT   ARCHITECT   AUGUST 25th 1940

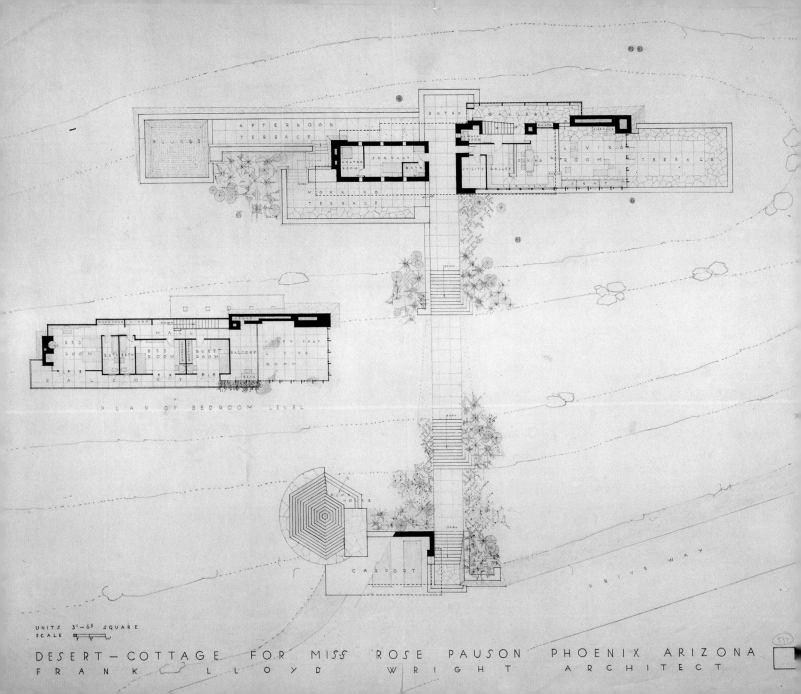

PLUNGE

AFTERNOON TERRACE

MORNING TERRACE

ENTRY GALLERY

LIVING ROOM

TERRACE

UTILITY GALLERY

PLAN OF BEDROOM LEVEL

BED ROOM

HALL

BED ROOM

GUEST ROOM

BALCONY

LIVING ROOM

BALCONY

SUMMER HOUSE

CARPORT

DRIVE WAY

UNITS 3'-6" SQUARE
SCALE

DESERT—COTTAGE FOR MISS ROSE PAUSON PHOENIX ARIZONA
FRANK LLOYD WRIGHT ARCHITECT

Photographs by Robert Mosher, October 1940

FRANK LLOYD WRIGHT

TALIESIN

NOVEMBER 29th, 1940

HERE WE ARE LIVING IN THE HOUSE AND WANT YOU TO KNOW THAT
WE ARE DELIGHTED WITH IT AND IT IS AS BEAUTIFUL AS YOU
PROMISED ME IT WOULD BE. HURRY OUT AND JOIN US.

                                    ROSE PAUSON

Dear Mr Wright —

We have been living in the house for
several days so I thought you might like
to hear a few further details —
Your designing of the house is perfectly
marvelous and I love every bit of it —
You will make history on one more front —
The only thing I regret very much and
I think you will feel the same way
about it is the carpenter work — To
say that it is bad is a gross understate
ment. We are now trying to stop up
places all over the house where the
wood work doesn't meet itself — Practically
all the flies in Arizona have found
the gaps and we have to spend most
of the day trying to fight them off —
Bob Mosher has been wonderful on the
job and I don't see how he ever
accomplished a house at all with
the many handicaps he must have
had to contend with — He has been most
helpful to me in every way —
When will you be here?
        Greetings to all
            Rose Pauson
Monday

Santa Fe

The Chief

My dear Rose Pauson —
So glad you are in your new home.
We will get together now and make it
fit you arriving end of this week.
The scheme of the house contemplated
shrinkage in the boards and after
several months exposure to the
sun the screws were all to be
tightened and the joints outside and
inside "painted" with a master head
laid on with a ~~gun~~ " Bobby must
have ~~explained~~ this? Of course there
would be open joints at first —
The same is true of the sanding of
rough edges and surfaces. This can
be done to any extent you desire.
We are going to move in some Tall
Saguaro' for you when the boys
arrive and do some other things.
~~Seems~~ to be some mix up about
"aero shades." They should be smooth

(over)

62

redwood splints.

I am sure we are all, eventually proud of your house. And I guess you can compare it favorably with any one in Phoenix costing twice or three times as much.

Looking forward to seeing you both "at home" soon

Faithfully,
FLLW

My Dear Rose Pauson,

So glad you are in your new home. We will get together now and make it fit; am arriving end of this week.

The scheme of the house contemplated shrinkage in the boards and after several months of exposure to the sun the screws were all to be tightened and the joints outside and inside to be "painted" with a mastic bead laid on with a "gun." Bobby must have explained this and of course there would be open joints at first.

The same is true of the sanding of rough edges and surfaces. This can be done to any extent you desire.

We are going to move in some tall "saguaro" for you when the boys arrive and do some other things. Seems to be some mishap about "aeroshades." They should be smooth redwood splints.

I am sure we are all, eventually proud of your house. And I guess you can compare it favorably with any one in Phoenix costing twice or three times as much.

Looking forward to seeing you both "at home" soon.
Faithfully,
FLLW

Dear Mr Wright –

Last Friday Mr. Ellis was here fixing the many leaks which appeared during the Christmas Eve storm – When I saw you yesterday I hoped that they had been successfully taken care of, so I didnt mention it to you –

Last night and today the rains poured in to the house again in so many places and so severely that I really feel not only discouraged but alarmed – It is a very serious situation for me – We were up at all hours during the night rescuing my possessions – Gertrude and I just wont be able to cope with it alone –

New Years Greetings to you all   Cordially

Rose Pauson

R 7 Box 457

Rose Pauson
Photograph by Helen Forbes, February 1941

Photograph by Johnny Green, winter 1941   Photograph by William Weiss, winter 1941

My dear Miss Rose:

Please do not worry about the "lien" so called.   I've read the text Gene brought and it is so completely false that you can land the young man in jail if you want to.

I am sorry you didn't get Matt Walton, a lawyer of highest standing here who knows the inns and outs of the peculiar place - as well.

Your Los Angeles man is too far away and will simply pick a correspondent here and action will be double back-action probably.   The "lien" means nothing more than that Ellis has the specified sum tied up to fight for and prove that he is entitled to it.   We should institute suit against him immediately ourselves for breach of contract and put him on the defensive - now.

I am afraid an old family lawyer will get everything too heavy and not effective. Sorry I am on my back. You should get Walton anyway and come up here soon as you can. I am arranging the papers so Matt Walton can oresent the case to your Los Angeles friend for advise if you elect.

Hastily and so sorry for your needless scare. After all, this is probably the best way to settle with this man Ellis. He is now in his own truly bad color.

Faithfully,

Frank Lloyd Wright
Taliesin West

February 6th, 1941

Note: It appears the contractor filed a lien in order to dispute his payment amount. Since Wright handled these negotiations on behalf of Pauson, Wright's letter implies his frustration with the contractor's method as it has upset his client.

Dear Mr Wright –

To night's storm is blowing and pouring into the house in such a way that unless something can be done about it I am afraid I shall have to move myself and my possessions out. The rain is pouring through the whole west wall and my clothes and everything on that side of the house had to be rescued – The entrance hall is under water and the shelves are practically a waterfall –

We have had to save the large door by nailing it but I have no idea what will happen between now and morning –

The rain is pouring through the rock work in the famous $100 closet and the wind is sailing through the whole house as if it were a tent –

I have tried to be very patient about the serious defects in the house but it just isn't a shelter at all in the bad weather – I am afraid that the amount of money

specified for fixing the house will not
even take care of the leaks, if they can
be fixed at all —

I feel very disturbed about the condition
of the house and I dont see how I can
accept it with such serious faults —

My greetings to all
very cordially,
Rose Pauson

Tuesday March fourth —

Photograph by Ambrose Whitmer, April 1941

70

MISS ROSE PAUSON:2510 JACKSON STREET:SAN FRANCISCO:CALIFORNIA

My dear Miss Rose: I hadn't thought of putting the house on a"strict
business basis" because I had intended to do what we could and charge you what
we were out of pocket plus something for our labor. But I guess you are right.
So the boys and I have made up a budget estimate of what we think the work will
cost and it is herewith, together with the drawings of what we propose to do.
You will read the drawings easily enough by now, I hope.   We will send you a regula
certificate of payment - the strict business - as we have to have the money as
the work progresses. I hope this is all sufficiently businesslike to meet your
views and your purse, too, in the very best Wright-Pauson tradition. If not,
let us know immediately so the boys may either stay or go.

I am leaving very soon myself but all is lined up.   I've been three times to
the house with the boys to get everything on straight.

On a strict business basis you owe your architect as follows:

10% of total cost of house on basis of arbitrator's report: $904.58
Apprentice services: May 1st to November 27th, after deducting
two months for probably idle TIME of apprentice in circumstances,   500.00
(See enclosed sheet for invariable basis of our practice)
                                                                  _____

TOTAL $1404.58

Paid to date: April 1938 $180.00
                February 1938   300.00
                September 1940   125.00
                November, 1940   175.00
                                 $780.00

TOTAL BALANCE DUE ARCHITECT TO DATE . . . . $ 624.58

No Architect's commission is charged on the following items: We are charging yo
for apprentice time only and cost of materials. For the materials used in correct
ing the house the sum will not exceed $150.00 probably. This leaves us to do the
work on the house correcting Ellis's mistakes ourselves without charge to you

except for the materials needed for the work. (It is however his privilege to do the work himself and collect the 480 if he chooses. I do not think he will do it, so we are proceeding.

In spite of the "strict business basis" I may mention the fact that you could not (except as we do it ourselves) get the features built (get the job done) for less than twice what we are undertaking to complete the work for. The total you will pay plus what materials will be needed to put the house in good condition will be:

Extension of carport roof	$170.00
PumpHouse and Storage space	480.00
Triplicate Terrace and steps	550.00
Total	$1200.00

Miss Gertrude said to me that she wished to share in the cost of the terraces so you might show her the drawings and estimates to see if she approves also.

Sincerely as always,

Frank Lloyd Wright
Taliesin West

April 29th, 1941

Dear Mr. Wright –

It was a great shock to me to realize by the tone and contents of your letter that you are very annoyed with me for desiring to work in a "business like way" – we seem to have a completely different idea of the meaning of the word "business like".

I have a very deep feeling of affection and friendship for you and Mrs Wright and I desired to protect that through avoiding further indefinite business arrangements – we both know that this was the mistake which caused me so much trouble

and extra expense that Mr. Ellis was not entirely responsible for – I now have the lawyers and arbitrators fees to add to this – I have been willing to pay for these mistakes with, I think you will agree, a minimum of complaint. However, I do not see how you can find it unreasonable of me to ~~try not to expect an impos~~ to expect to have some information about what I am going to spend –

The matter of the apprentice fees has at no previous time been mentioned to me verbally or in writing – The brochure which you inclose was never presented to me before – The two checks which I sent to Bob Mosher were, as

far as I knew, under the item of architects fees as there was
no other architects supervision during construction
This is the kind of situation between us which
I was trying to avoid when I spoke of proceeding
in a "business like way" - $

I feel that your contribution can never be
translated into terms of money - I hope you know
that - I wish I could return something
do you that would be adequate, but it never could
be money - Very sincerely
Rose Pauson

May second -

FJ51 33 NT 4 EXTRA= DUPE OF FONED TGM= SPRINGGREN WIS MAY 13

ROSE PAUSON=

2510 JACKSON ST=

DEAR ROSE PAUSON: NO OFFENSE TAKEN OR INTENDED. YOU ARE
RIGHT. PLEASE SEND OK TO HALSTEAD LUMBER COMPANY PHOENIX
AUTHORIZING US TO ORDER MATERIALS FOR WORK AT YOUR HOUSE=
FRANK LLOYD WRIGHT.

76

DEAR MISS ROSE:

Concerning your inquiry about a supervision fee...
as I have nothing whatsoever to do with matters between the architect and his client, consequently no
mention of this has been made to me, I can answer
only in a non-committal manner. When I first saw
the preliminary sketches I wanted to work on the
house, I stayed down in the Desert that first summer
solely for that purpose but nothing happened so I
stayed the second summer. I just wanted to build it,
thats all, and guess nothing else mattered. My only
regret is that I didn't do a better job of it.

Such apprentice payments are always made not to the
apprentice but to Mr Wright directly and relayed in
part to us by him; our function is solely confined
to the building, nothing else, so that I know little
 of what transpires between Mr Wright and his client,
my feelings donot enter the picture. Such payments
that you sent to me while building the house were
under Mr Wright's order to be used by me for running
expenses at camp, not for me personally. As for me
I personally feel that there are no obligations to
me whatsoever.

Sincerely,

Bob

June 12th 1941

MISS ROSE PAUSON: 2510 JACKSON STREET:SAN FRANCISCO:CALIFORNIA

My dear Miss Rose: The work on the house is about done. We can finally
settle for that when you see it and be satisfied.   Meantime I wonder if
you couldn't help us by paying the architect and getting rid of him. Since
I failed to get it over to you that the apprentice had to be paid superintendence
instead of general supervision included in plans we will cut that in two again --
reducing the balance due him by $250.00. Balance then $374.58.

I hope you are as fine as fine can be.   My best to Miss Gertrude and all your
friends.

Faithfully,

Frank Lloyd Wright
July 2nd, 1941

Rose Pauson by the fireplace, 1941

Dear Mr Wright —

I have just been looking
over the bills and checks
that I have here with me
and perhaps I am not the
good business man that
you accused me of being —
What I am able to find is
this — two cancelled checks
from Blaine, $600 and one
bill which says 'hauling,
stone and gravel, labor'.
You asked me during the

summer for a duplicate for your
files so you must have the other
one —
I also have cancelled checks
from Halsteads — I am sending
you the tags I can find so that
you can see it includes all
kinds of materials — cement,
lumber, canvas, nails, oils
etc — all materials used were
paid by me except the stone
and gravel — according to
what I can find this
amounts to $911.42 including
Blaines bill — I can't find

how I arrived at the figure I thought
I had paid and that I mentioned this
morning – This is all I can prove and
I must have added some other expenditure.
It may be a mix up between Gertrude and me.

    Christmas Greetings to all the family
        Cordially
          Rose

Monday

Gertrude Pauson
Photograph by Sherwood Smith, 1941

My dear Miss Rose: It must be "hell" to be a "business man" and at the
same time love beauty! No one yet, so far as I know, ever got out of life alive
with that.   Gene reports difficulty in getting you to comprehend the simple
fact that $450.00 was allowed to put your house into the order your architect
considered just, and that this sum of money, by right, should have gone into *MS*
for putting the house back into the shape it should have been in - in the first
place - according to your architect's judgement. Now your architect doesn't
deliver houses complete according to a possibly whimsical client's wishes. And
in work such as we have done on your house about 2/3rds of the cost, always, is
labor. About 1/3rd is for materials.

In making an estimate of the new work, plus putting the house into good order,
the Fellowship balked at the estimate of $1,350.00 I proposed to them. They
said that they sum knocked off the settlement for putting the house in good order
should be added to the estimate of $1,200.00 making it $1650.00 and also that
an architect's fee should be added which would make the total $1770.00. This
would have been the "business-like" basis of the sum I proposed to you and that
you would have gladly accepted because that sum would be, in toto, less than
the new work itself would have cost you in any case - and did cost us if labor
is worth anything at all.

Apparently you didn't think ours worth much. But I disagree. The work done
by the Fellowship on your home is better done than the professional contractor
could or would do it. The money I proposed you pay for the house ($1350.00)
does not really entitle you to the kind of workmanship to which you seem to
believe yourself entitled for some reason that I fail to comprehend.

Now, in recognition of your friendly appreciation of the difficulty encountered
in getting anything at all done, even as well as the rough-wood type of construction specified did require - I proposed to take no more than $150.00 out of
the $450.00 allowed by arbitration to fix up the house, leaving you the rest.
To salvage your wounded feelings?   But you refuse to appreciate or even
understand this now. Why?

Then, too, feeling our superintendence faulty I made further amends by throwing in the architect's fees on your new work. This left us only $1350.00 to do what should and would have cost you more than double that sum in any other circumstances whatever. The materials in the work came to $878.58 (deducting (although I don't know why) the $125.00 for food that went into the workers to enable them to work. So three times that sum should and would have been in other circumstances the contract price you would have been asked to pay - or $2,635.74. Yet you are not content?

Now, also, by paying the material bills yourself (according to a letter from Blaine, was an arrangement apparently effected by you with Halstead) you robbed the boys of the 20% on materials a contractor (the Fellowship in this case) is entitled to receive which seems to me somewhat mean and got you nothing at all. But pass that on to you as a "good business man". (I believe "good-business" is usually like that) and let us fact the fact that (two senior and one junior) apprentices working on your building in hot summer- time would receive, for several month's earnest labor - and competent labor, I say - (if you paid in full $1,350.00 the reduced figure I proposed to you) - $346.42 and nothing at all for the designs and details or profit on their labor. In other words, and finally, about one third the regular cost to you in ordinary circumstances.

Knowing this, that you should object to this contract which I made with you, serves me right do you think? To keep the letter of any contract is "business is business". And I do not feel that any argument I make will take the bandage off the eyes of "Justice" in this case if you, Miss Rose, are Justice. But there is more than Justice involved. Do you want Justice? I think not. Mercy all around is all we can get or give and a lot better than Justice... especially at Christmas-tide.

Where or what materials went intothe work done for you is not your business, if business is business." And the fact that we are still working to stop a few minor-leaks and fix a sash or two should in all conscience have no bearing on whether you pay up your contract now and show your good faith or not.

A woman's fear of imposition or desertion in the circumstances I assure you
has not nor will affect the issue. We merely ask to be met in the spirit
in which we have served you. We were not asking enough, as you may see from
the facts I submit to you here.

But we will clean up our bit. Meantime we hold the bag and leave you to think
it over.

Sincerely,

Frank Lloyd Wright
December 23rd, 1941

N.B. For the time and trouble I have taken in writing this to you I could
have turned in to my publishers material for which I would receive twice ~~that~~
the sum in dispute. So how foolish the whole thing is ——

TALIESIN WEST • PHOENIX ARIZONA

Dear Mr. Wright –

You asked me to think over your letter and I have been thinking a great deal. I feel that your letter is as unjust and insulting as Mrs. Murdocks' letter.

I am sure that I do not need to defend myself of the accusation that I have robbed the Fellowship – You also accuse me of having

effected an arrangement with Halstead unknown to you – I have a letter at home which will prove that to be untrue –

You might be happy to hear that I have not gotten off too cheaply with the work and what I actually have paid is closer to the Fellowships figures than to yours – I had to replace the motor on my pump ($85) plus the work in connection with that, due to mishandling during construction on the pump house – I also paid for Eddie's labor during that period and several other bills for which I can offer you no proof until I have access to my papers in San Francisco –

If you will send me a bill or statement saying that my account has been paid in full, I shall be glad to exchange it for $150 and consider the work finished –
Your whimsical client
Rose Pauson
December 30, 1941 Phoenix Arizona –

Rose Pauson

TALIESIN WEST • PHOENIX ARIZONA

My dear Miss Rose: My letters should never be written on the spur
of the moment as I am under terrific pressure these days and they are likely t
to be acrimonious when in a day or two the heat would be turned off and a
better view taken. I was provoked that the terms I stated as clearly as I ~~you~~
could should have again made confusion. And I felt put out that our really
extraordinary efforts - such as we are - in behalf of your "opus" should be
tallied so severely and (as I thought when I wrote), grudgingly. But I
see that is not true.

No doubt the shoe pinches you as mine does me. And my "whimsical client"
was hypothetical as you will see if you will read the line again. It
is hardest always to work for those *satisfactorily to whom* ~~which~~ actual knowledge of work-values
cannot be adequate.

But I see your side just the same. The Fellowship will ask no more money
of you until the leaky places that remain are fixed. Then you may pay us $
$150.00 in full satisfaction of our claims. We will send you two sahuaros

to seal the release and we will all heave a sigh of relief and I hope, satisfaction.

We want to see the house when it is raining. Two boys are ready to come down this morning after last night's square wind and wet. I thought your Mexican boy was caretaker, staying there anyway, and helped, just naturally. Blaine said the pump "blow-out" was his (the boy's) affair. But, how do we know?

I am slowly learning my lessons, like a tough boy in a hard school.

" I hope you are the same."

We have appreciated the appreciation and friendship of "the Pausons" as you have every reason, I think, to know.

If that passes out, it will not be our fault.

Faithfully,
Frank Lloyd Wright
Frank Lloyd Wright
January 2, 1942

92

Dear Mr. Wright —

Thank you for your letter and also for your generous offer of two suharos — I would like to have you see the present planting first as we have taken down the tall suhuaro and filled the space with other desert plants —

I don't know why you think I havent appreciated the Fellowship efforts and certainly any loss of friendship there would cause me only unhappiness —

My greetings to you all not whimsically (I hope) but cordially

Rose Pauson

Tuesday —

Dear Mr. Wright —

Sunday evening the unhappy news reached me that our Phoenix house had burned down — at five o'clock that morning — It was completely destroyed, including everything that had been stored in the little fireproof closet on the balcony —

I need not express to you my own feelings on the destruction of so much beauty because I know that you will feel as I do — It was so much more than a material possession —

I have at the present time no further information nor do I know the origin of the fire —

My warmest greetings to you and Mrs Wright —

Cordially

Rose

Thursday —

WESTERN UNION

1201

The filing time shown in the date line on telegrams and day letters is STANDARD TIME at point of origin. Time of receipt is STANDARD TIME at point of destination

SA1344 7 NL=SPRINGGREEN WIS 19   1943 APR 19 PM 10 45

ROSE PAUSON=

2510 JACKSON ST SFRAN=

SHOCKED AND MYSTIFIED. INVESTIGATION SHOULD BE THOROUGH=

FRANK LLOYD WRIGHT.

Fi - 1638 add
Ut 836a mailed

95

Photograph courtesy Robert McMahan Photography